D1264707

Vietnamese Foods & Culture

by Jennifer Ferro

The Rourke Press, Inc.
Vero Beach, FL 32964

Note to Readers: The recipes in this book are meant to be enjoyed by young people. Children should ask an adult for help, however, when preparing any recipe involving knives, blenders, or other sharp implements and the use of stoves, microwaves, or other heating appliances.

On the Cover: *Vietnamese people burn red sticks of incense to bring good luck on Tet.*

Photo Credits: Cover photo AP/Wide World Photos; p. 4 Eyewire; p. 6 CORBIS/ Catherine Karnow; p. 9, 10, 25 Lou Dematteis; p. 12, 24, 36 PhotoDisc; p. 13 CORBIS/ Michael S. Yamashita; p. 21, 31, 42 Paul O'Connor; p. 37 Omni-Photo/Robert Knopes; p. 38 CORBIS/Owen Franken.

Produced by Salem Press, Inc.

Library of Congress Cataloging-in-Publication Data

Ferro, Jennifer. 1968-
  Vietnamese foods and culture / Jennifer Ferro.
   p.   cm. — (Festive foods & celebrations)
  Includes index.
  Summary: Discusses some of the foods enjoyed in Vietnam and describes special foods that are part of such specific celebrations as Tet, Wandering Souls Day, and the Mid-Autumn Festival. Includes recipes.
  ISBN 1-57103-306-8
  1. Cookery, Vietnamese Juvenile literature. 2. Food habits—Vietnam Juvenile literature. 3. Festivals—Vietnam Juvenile literature. [1. Food habits—Vietnam. 2. Cookery, Vietnamese. 3. Festivals—Vietnam. 4. Holidays—Vietnam. 5. Vietnam— Social life and customs.] I. Title. II. Series: Ferro, Jennifer. 1968-   Festive foods & celebrations.
TX724.5.V5F47   1999
641.59597—dc21   99-24325
                                                                                CIP

First Printing

PRINTED IN THE UNITED STATES OF AMERICA

Contents

Introduction to Vietnam

Vietnam (vee-et-NOM) is a country in the southeast part of the *continent* (KON-tih-nunt) of *Asia* (AY-zhuh). It is beneath China and *borders* the South China Sea.

People who live there are called Vietnamese (vee-ut-nuh-MEEZ). They say their country is shaped like a *bamboo* pole with a bucket of rice at each end. Vietnam has mountains, jungles, forests, sea coasts, and rivers.

In the past, many other countries have ruled

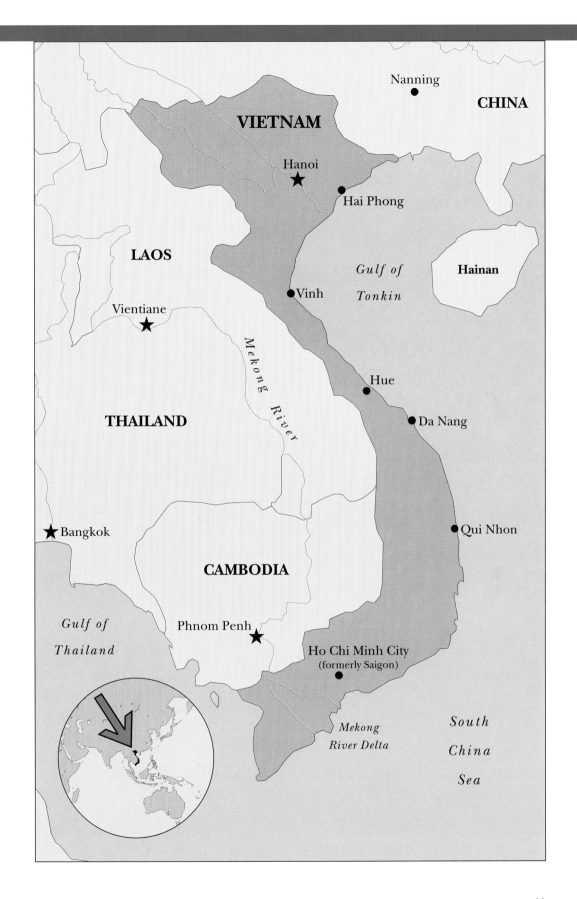

A teenage girl rides a motorcycle in the city of Hanoi.

Vietnam. Mongolia, China, and France are some of them. For many years, it was part of a *colony* (KALL-uh-nee) called French Indochina.

In 1954, the country was divided in half. The north was run under a system called *communism.* North Vietnam and South Vietnam fought a war against each other. The United States fought on the side of South Vietnam. In 1975, the north won the war. Today, Vietnam is one country again.

Not many people in Vietnam own cars. Most of them get around on motorcycles, bicycles, or tricycles that carry people in the back called cyclos.

Most Vietnamese people follow a religion called Buddhism (BOO-dih-zum). It is based on the teachings of the *Buddha* (BOO-duh). He was a *philosopher* in India who lived more than two thousand years ago. Vietnamese Buddhism is special. It is mixed with ideas from other religions called Confucianism (kun-FYOO-shuh-nih-zum) and Taoism (DOW-ih-zum).

People in Vietnam believe that their dead grandparents and other family members watch over them. Dead relatives are called ancestors (AN-sess-turz). Every home has an altar to remember the family's ancestors. An altar is an area where candles and pictures of ancestors are placed.

Vietnamese people believe that numbers can bring good luck or bad luck. The numbers 13 and 3 are always unlucky. People think it is unlucky to live at an address with 13 in it. The number 9 is lucky. Everyone wants to live at an address with 9 in it. Other lucky numbers depend on the time, day, and year of your birth.

Vietnam has warm, *humid* weather. Many kinds of *tropical* (TRAW-pih-kull) fruits grow in this type of weather. Vietnamese people eat a lot of fresh fruit and vegetables in their meals.

French bread and coffee were brought to Vietnam when France ruled the country. Today

Young children bring flowers to a statue of communist leader Ho Chi Minh.

Rice is grown in areas of wet land called paddies.

Vietnamese people still bake French bread and make sandwiches with it.

Vietnamese people do not use forks, knives, or spoons. They eat with chopsticks. Chopsticks are two thin sticks made of wood that you hold together in one hand. You can use chopsticks to pick up foods like noodles and rice.

Rice is served at every meal in Vietnam. Rice is a grain from a tall grass that grows in 4 inches of water. It is grown in areas called *rice paddies.*

Vietnamese people eat a couple of different kinds of rice. One type is called jasmine rice. The grains of rice stick together when they are cooked. It is easy to pick up sticky rice with chopsticks.

Tet

New Year in Vietnam is called Tet Nguyen-Den (tet nyi-EN den) or just Tet. It is the biggest holiday in the country. Tet is celebrated for seven days in Vietnam. It marks the beginning of the new calendar year and the birth of spring.

Vietnamese people follow a *lunar* calendar. It is different from the one used in Western countries like the United States. Tet happens during January, February, or March on Western calendars. Chinese people follow the same calendar as

Vietnamese people. They celebrate the New Year on the same day.

Vietnamese people believe that *gods* live in their kitchens and protect their homes. The kitchen gods leave the house seven days before Tet. They go to tell Heaven if the family was good or bad

Two men use a puppet to perform the Lion Dance for Tet.

that year. People try to scare away evil spirits while the gods are away. They set off *firecrackers* and make loud noises.

Everything is about luck on Tet. Vietnamese people believe you will be lucky all year if you have good luck on the first day of the New Year. You will be unlucky all year if you have bad luck on the first day.

Many things are done to make sure a family has good luck on Tet. Brand-new money is given

Birth Signs

Years in Vietnam and China are named after one of 12 animals—rat, ox, tiger, cat, dragon, snake, horse, goat, monkey, rooster, dog, or pig. Every animal has its own personality. Some animals are mean. Some are very smart. Some are physically strong. Others are hardworking. Vietnamese people believe that the animal year you are born in makes you like that animal. This is called your birth sign. Chinese people use these animals to mark their years too.

to children in bright red envelopes. Adults get gifts of food like *mangoes, papayas,* coffee, and chocolate.

Vietnamese people believe that all their debts must be paid by the New Year. Otherwise, they will have bad luck. They return borrowed things. They buy new clothes to look their best for the New Year. These are signs of good luck.

People clean their houses one week before Tet. No cleaning is done on Tet because the good luck might be swept away.

Families see the most important person in their lives on the first day of the New Year. They see other important people on the rest of the days. The first person on the first day of Tet brings either good luck or bad luck for the whole year. Some families who have bad luck blame their first visitor on last year's Tet.

On New Year's Day, a long colorful *dragon* walks through the streets. It is really a big puppet moved by many people inside. Families believe they will have good luck and lots of money if the dragon dances in front of their house.

Special foods are eaten during Tet. They eat squares of rice wrapped in banana leaves. These squares take hours to prepare. Also, dishes are made with fresh spring vegetables, like asparagus soup.

Birthdays are not celebrated in Vietnam. A child is considered one year old at birth. The child turns two years old when Tet comes. Everyone in the country turns one year older on Tet.

Asparagus Soup

1 egg

1/2 pound of fresh asparagus

1 boneless, skinless chicken breast

2 tablespoons of cornstarch

1/4 cup of water

2 cups or 1 14-ounce can of chicken broth

2 teaspoons of soy sauce

◆ Crack the egg into a small bowl. Beat it lightly.

◆ Chop the asparagus and chicken breast into bite-sized pieces.

◆ Mix the cornstarch and water in another small bowl. Stir until it forms a sticky paste.

- Pour the chicken broth into a large saucepan. Turn the heat on high. Bring it to a *boil*.

- Add the asparagus. Turn the heat down to medium. Cover and cook for 3 minutes.

- Add the chicken. Cook for 4 minutes.

- Add the cornstarch mixture and soy sauce. Stir until the soup starts to thicken, just a few minutes.

- Stir in the egg a little at a time. Cook for 30 more seconds.

- Pour over rice. Or serve small bowls of rice on the side. Serves 4.

Glass Noodle Salad

1 6-ounce package of rice noodles or bean
  threads

1 tomato, seeded and chopped

2 carrots

1 stem of lemon grass

1 bunch of cilantro

2 cloves of garlic

1/2 onion

2 tablespoons of vegetable oil

1/4 teaspoon of pepper

1/4 teaspoon of chile pepper flakes

2 cups of shredded cabbage

1 pound of shrimp, cooked and shelled
  (or beef or chicken)

1 tablespoon of soy sauce

◆ Place the rice noodles into a large bowl.
  Pour boiling water on top. Soak for 15

minutes. Drain. Chop the noodles in half.

- Cut the tomato in half. Scoop out the seeds. Chop the tomato into pieces. Peel the carrots. Cut them into thin strips.

- Peel off the outer layers of the lemon grass. Chop the inside stalk into very small pieces. Cut the stems off the cilantro. Throw them away. Chop the leaves into small pieces.

- Peel the garlic. Chop the cloves into small pieces. Cut the onion in half. Peel off the skin and outer layer. Cut an onion half into thin slices.

- Heat the oil in a skillet. Add the garlic

and onions. Wait until they start to turn golden. Add the lemon grass, pepper, and chile pepper flakes.

♦ Add the shrimp. (You can also use very thin slices of beef or chicken.) Cook for

Glass Noodle Salad

a few seconds, until they are hot. Stir.
Add the soy sauce.

♦ Divide the noodles, carrots, cabbage,
  and tomatoes into bowls. Spoon the
  shrimp or meat mixture on top.
  Serves 4.

Vietnamese Bananas

2 bananas
2 tablespoons of butter or margarine
2 tablespoons of firmly packed brown
  sugar, light or dark
4 scoops of coconut ice cream

♦ Peel the bananas. Cut them into
  1/2-inch slices.

- Melt the butter or margarine in a large skillet over medium heat.

- Stir in the brown sugar with a wooden spoon. Make sure all the lumps are out.

- Add the banana slices to the pan. Cook until they are lightly browned. Turn them over. Cook on the other side until they are lightly browned.

- Scoop the ice cream into bowls. Top it with warm bananas. Serves 4.

Wandering Souls Day

In Vietnam, death is very important. It is seen as a chance to go on to a nicer life. When people die, family members set up altars for them and other ancestors in their homes.

An altar is an area in the house where pictures of a family's ancestors are placed. Candles are lit there. Incense is burned for the dead spirits. Incense is a stick of *herbs* that burns very slowly. It gives off a small stream of scented smoke.

Relatives celebrate the anniversary of an

Village elders perform a ceremony to honor ancestors at a local temple.

ancestor's death. They place favorite foods of the ancestor on the altar. They pray to the altar to remember and honor the ancestors.

Wandering Souls Day takes place in August. It is a day to honor the ancestors who have no families to pray for them. It is also called Ancestor Death Day.

Food is very important in celebrating the ancestors. People start to prepare different

Fish Sauce

Fish sauce is used in Vietnamese cooking. It is also eaten in Cambodia (kam-BO-dee-uh) and Thailand (TIE-land). These countries are neighbors of Vietnam. Fish sauce is made from *fermenting*, or rotting, fish. Small fish called anchovies are put in large wooden barrels. After six months, they are pressed with a board. Juice comes out of the fish. This juice is poured into bottles. It is very salty like soy sauce. Fish sauce is used instead of salt in most Vietnamese dishes.

Coconut Milk

Coconuts are the fruit of the coconut palm tree. This tree can grow to be 100 feet tall. Coconuts grow in bunches under the leaves at the top of the tree. If you see a coconut in a grocery store, shake it to hear the water inside. This is called coconut water. Some people drink it. Coconut milk is made from the tough, white meat on the inside the coconut. First the hard brown shell is cracked with a hammer. Then the white meat is grated with a special coconut grater. Milk is made by *grinding* this meat. Coconut milk is used in a lot of Vietnamese recipes.

dishes two days before Wandering Souls Day.

On Wandering Souls Day, all the food is placed on the altar. Three sticks of incense are lit. Everyone bows three times to the altar. Then the door is opened to invite in the spirits or souls of the ancestors. No one is allowed to eat until the incense has gone out.

Stir-Fry Vegetables

4 carrots

any other vegetables

2 cloves of garlic

1 tablespoon of vegetable oil

2 cups of broccoli

1 cup bean sprouts

1 cup shredded cabbage

1 tablespoon of soy sauce

- Peel the carrots. Chop them into large pieces. Chop any other vegetables you want into large pieces.

- Peel the garlic. Chop the cloves into small pieces.

- Heat the oil on medium-high in a large skillet.

- Add the garlic. Wait until it starts to sizzle. Add the carrots, broccoli, bean sprouts, cabbage, and any other vegetables. Stir with a wooden spoon.

♦ Cook for 7 minutes. Take the pan off the heat quickly so the vegetables do not get soggy.

♦ Add the soy sauce. Stir. Serve over bowls of white rice. Serves 4.

Spring Rolls

Rice paper wrappers are made of rice flour pressed into a very thin round shape and dried. They are white and can be eaten raw. They are sold in Thai, Vietnamese, or Cambodian stores. You can also use the egg and flour wrappers that Chinese people use for egg rolls.

3 ounces of rice noodles

3 carrots

3 green onions (scallions)

1 egg

1 pound of ground pork or beef

2 teaspoons of fish sauce or soy sauce

1 package of rice paper wrappers or
round egg roll wrappers

1/2 cup of vegetable oil

- Place the rice noodles into a large bowl. Pour boiling water on top. Soak for 15 minutes. Drain. Chop the noodles into small pieces.

- Peel the carrots. Cut them into thin strips. Chop the green onions into very thin slices.

- Crack the egg into a large bowl. Beat it lightly. Add the meat, carrots, green onions, fish or soy sauce, and rice noodles.

◆ Soak the rice paper wrappers one at a time in a bowl of very warm water. Place a wrapper on a kitchen towel. Add a heaping tablespoon of meat mixture just below the center. Fold the bottom up. Fold the sides in. Roll from the bottom up. Repeat until the wrappers and mixture are gone.

Spring Rolls, Rice, and Dipping Sauce

- ◆ Heat the oil in a large skillet on medium. Wait about 1 minute. Add 4 rolls into the pan. Make sure each one touches the bottom and does not stick to the others.

- ◆ Fry until golden brown, about 10 minutes. Turn to brown the other side. Serve with dipping sauce (see the following recipe).

Nuoc Cham

This dipping sauce is used like salt.

2 cloves of garlic
juice from 1/2 of a lime
1 teaspoon of red pepper flakes
2 tablespoons of sugar
4 tablespoons of fish sauce or soy sauce
1 cup of water

- Peel the garlic. Crush the cloves in a garlic press. Or chop them into very tiny pieces. Place the garlic into a bowl.

- Cut a lime in half. Stick a fork into the middle. Twist it around over the bowl to squeeze the juice out.

- Add the red pepper flakes, sugar, fish or soy sauce, and water. Stir until the sugar dissolves.

- The sauce can be left in the refrigerator for up to 2 weeks. Makes 1 1/2 cups.

Chicken Pho

This national soup of Vietnam is usually made with beef.

2 boneless, skinless chicken breasts
2 cans of chicken broth

10 button or brown mushrooms

1 6-ounce package of bean thread
   noodles or vermicelli pasta

1 bunch of cilantro

4 green onions (scallions)

4 ounces of bean sprouts

- Place the chicken breasts in a saucepan
  of boiling water. Cook for 10 minutes,
  until the middle is solid white. Remove.
  Chop into thin strips. Place the chicken
  into a bowl.

- Dump out all but 2 tablespoons of the
  water. Add the chicken broth. Turn the
  heat to medium.

- Chop the mushrooms into thin slices.
  Add them to the broth. Pour the broth
  into a bowl when it is hot.

- Put the bean threads into a bowl. Pour boiling water on top. Soak for 15 minutes. For vermicelli or other pasta, cook according to the directions on the box. Drain the noodles. Divide them into bowls.

- Cut the stems off the cilantro. Throw them away. Chop the leaves into pieces. Put them into a bowl.

- Put the bean sprouts into a bowl.

- Chop the green onions into small pieces, including the greens. Put them into a bowl.

- Serve the bowls of noodles. Add green onions, bean sprouts, cilantro, and chicken. Ladle the broth on top to make a soup. Serves 4.

Mid-Autumn Festival

The Mid-Autumn Festival is called Tet Trung Thu (tet trung too). Autumn (AW-tum) is another word for the season of fall. This festival happens in the eighth month of the year when the Moon is brightest. It began as a farming festival to celebrate the *harvest*. Today it is a holiday for children.

On the day of the festival, families tell young people the *legend* of a boy named Chu Cuoi. This story teaches children to listen to their

1,000-Year-Old Eggs

Some Vietnamese recipes call for 1,000-year-old eggs. These duck eggs only seem 1,000 years old. They are buried in fine ash, clay, and salt for about 100 days. The egg whites turn black and the yolks turn a gray-green. The eggs end up looking like pretty black marbles. People boil them in water before eating them. Sometimes they use them raw in dishes like moon cakes.

1,000-Year-Old Eggs

Mushrooms

Mushrooms are *spores* that grow on trees or in damp places. Vietnamese people use a lot of mushrooms in their cooking. One type is called tree ear or cloud ear mushrooms. These mushrooms grow on live or dying trees. Cloud ear mushrooms do not have much flavor. Instead, they take on the flavors of the foods they are cooked with. Cloud ear mushrooms are small and black. They are dried. They look like burnt and wrinkled pieces of paper. The mushrooms puff up like little clouds when they are soaked in liquid.

Women select mushrooms to sell in the market.

parents and to always tell the truth.

One day, Chu Cuoi was asked to guard a sacred tree. The tree was supposed to stay on Earth. But the boy did not respect the tree. He did some bad things to it. The tree began to tremble. It pulled itself out of the ground toward Heaven.

Chu Cuoi grabbed the roots. He tried to keep the tree on Earth. But the tree pulled him to the moon. You can see him on the night the moon is brightest. There the boy sits longing for home.

Children memorize the story of Chu Cuoi. They will tell it to their own children someday. This is how *traditions* are kept alive from year to year.

Two types of cakes are made for this festival— moon cakes and earth cakes. Eating them together is a symbol for the joining of Heaven and Earth in the legend of Chu Cuoi.

People also make lanterns from bamboo and paper. They are in the shapes of stars, the moon, boats, dragons, fish, lobsters, and other animals. The lanterns are carried in a parade with children following behind.

Sticky Rice with Peanuts and Raisins

1 cup of glutinous rice
   (a short-grain sweet rice)

1/2 cup of coconut milk

1/4 cup of sugar

1/2 teaspoon of salt

1/2 cup of raisins

1/2 cup of peanuts

◆ Soak the rice in a bowl of water for 2 hours. Drain.

◆ Fill a pan 1/4 full with water. Place a metal colander or vegetable strainer on top. Add the rice. (Line with cheesecloth if the rice falls through.) Make sure the rice does not touch the water. Cover.

◆ Bring the water to a boil. Steam the rice for 30 minutes. Spoon it into a bowl.

- Stir in the coconut milk, sugar, salt, and raisins.

- Serve with peanuts sprinkled on top. Serves 4.

Vietnamese Pancakes

These omelettes are poured to be very thin, like pancakes.

3 eggs
2 teaspoons of fish sauce or soy sauce
1/2 bunch of fresh cilantro
1/2 bunch of fresh mint
1 tablespoon of vegetable oil
10 small shelled, cooked shrimp

- Crack the eggs into a bowl. Add the fish or soy sauce. Beat until bubbly.

- Cut the stems off the cilantro and mint. Throw them away. Chop the leaves into pieces.

- Heat the oil in a skillet over medium heat.

- Pour in some egg mixture. Coat the bottom of pan thinly. Shake it so the pancake does not burn. Flip the pancake over with a spatula when only the center is still watery. Remove. Repeat with the rest of the batter.

- Serve the pancakes with the cilantro, mint, and shrimp. Serves 2.

Vietnamese Pancakes

Glossary

Asia: a large continent that has such countries as China, India, and Vietnam.

bamboo: tall, hard grass that grows like a tube.

boil: to heat water or another liquid until it starts to bubble.

border: the line that marks where one country ends and another begins.

Buddha: the founder the Eastern religion called Buddhism. He lived in India more than two thousand years ago.

colony: a country that is ruled by another country.

communism: a form of government in which the state owns all the businesses.

continent: a large body of land separated from other bodies of land by an ocean or sea. There are seven continents in the world.

dragon: a huge creature that looks like a giant lizard.

ferment: a chemical reaction in foods.

firecracker: a paper toy that is lit with a match to make a loud noise.

gods: beings that are thought to have special powers.

grind: to make into a powder.

harvest: the time of year when foods are ripe and ready to be picked.

herbs: plants that have strong flavors are used in cooking.

humid: damp or moist weather.

legend: a story that has been passed down for many years.

lunar: having to do with the moon.

mango: a sweet fruit eaten in Vietnam. It has yellow flesh and a large pit inside.

papaya: fruit that can grow to be very large. Some people it them green or unripe. They have many small, black seeds inside.

philosopher: someone who thinks about ways of looking at the world.

rice paddies: large areas of water where rice is grown.

soak: to cover in water and leave for a period of
   time.

spore: a type of organism like a mushroom.

traditions: things that happens the same way for
   many years.

tropical: areas of the world that are near the equator
   and have warm, wet weather.

Bibliography

Angell, Carole S. *Celebrations Around the World: A Multicultural Handbook.* Golden, Colo.: Fulcrum Press, 1996.

Cole, Wendy M. *Vietnam.* Philadelphia: Chelsea House, 1999.

Kindersley, Anabel, and Barnabas Kindersley. *Celebrations: Festivals, Carnivals, and Feast Days from Around the World.* New York: DK Publishing, 1997.

McKay, Susan. *Vietnam.* Singapore: Times Editions, 1997.

Nguyen, Chi, and Judy Monroe. *Cooking the Vietnamese Way.* Minneapolis: Lerner Publications, 1985.

O'Connor, Karen. *A Ticket to Vietnam.* Minneapolis: Carolrhoda Books, 1999.

Roop, Peter, and Connie Roop. *A Visit to Vietnam.* Oxford, England: Heinemann Library, 1998.

Seah, Audrey. *Vietnam.* New York: Marshall

Cavendish, 1999.

Webb, Lois Sinaiko. *Holidays of the World Cookbook for Students.* Phoenix, Ariz.: Oryx Press, 1995.

Wright, David K. *Vietnam.* Chicago: Children's Press, 1989.

websites:

http://www.holidayfestival.com

http://kicon.com

Index